Peter Hall

Born in 1930, Peter Hall went to school and university in Cambridge before embarking on a career as a theatre director. After débuts at Windsor and Oxford, he ran the Arts Theatre in London, where he directed the English-language world première of *Waiting for Godot*. After working at Stratford with Peggy Ashcroft, Laurence Olivier and Charles Laughton, he founded the Royal Shakespeare Company in 1960, for which he directed eighteen plays, including *The Wars of the Roses*, as well as premières of plays by Harold Pinter, Edward Albee and others at the RSC's London home, established by Hall at the Aldwych Theatre.

In 1973 Peter Hall was appointed to succeed Laurence Olivier as Director of the National Theatre. During his fifteen years there, he moved the Company to its present three-theatre building and directed the premières of, among others, *Amadeus, No Man's Land* and *Betrayal*, as well as notable productions of Aeschylus, Marlowe, Shakespeare and Jonson. On leaving the National he launched the Peter Hall Company with productions of *Orpheus Descending* with Vanessa Redgrave and *The Merchant of Venice* with Dustin Hoffman, followed by many other productions including *An Ideal Husband,* Stephen Dillane as Hamlet, *School for Wives, An Absolute Turkey, Lysistrata* and *A Streetcar Named Desire* with Jessica Lange.

In 1997 he presided over a landmark season of thirteen plays with a permanent Company at the Old Vic, relocating the following year to the Piccadilly. The productions included *Waiting for Godot, Waste, The Misanthrope, Major Barbara* and *Filumena* with Judi Dench.

Sir Peter is also a renowned opera director (he was artistic director of Glyndebourne from 1984 to 1990) and has directed feature films and television drama. He published his *Diaries* in 1983 and his autobiography, *Making an Exhibition of Myself*, in 1993.

Also in the Dramatic Contexts series

Aristotle   *Poetics*
Peter Brook   *Evoking Shakespeare*

Peter Hall

The
Necessary
Theatre

Theatre Communications Group
New York

The Necessary Theatre is published by
Theatre Communications Group,
355 Lexington Avenue, New York, NY 10017.

This edition is published in an arrangement with
Nick Hern Books.

A CIP catalog record for this book is available on file
at the Library of Congress.

ISBN 1-55936-178-6

First U.S. edition, September 1999

Typeset by Country Setting, Kingsdown, Kent CT14 8ES
Printed and bound in Great Britain by Cox and Wyman,
Reading, Berks

Foreword

This little book is very much of its moment –
1999. It makes the case for subsidy at a time when
it is no longer thought fashionable or necessary,
and when New Labour is busy restructuring and
deforming the arts, while congratulating itself that
it encourages them. The gap between reality and
sharp public relations is the mark of *fin de siècle*
in Britain.

My book also makes the case for theatre
companies. New developments in the theatre have
always come out of a consistent period of group
work. As I write this, there are no real companies left
in Britain. They too are unfashionable – principally
because they cost money. Yet I believe that a
subsidised company is the foundation of a healthy
theatre. And without a healthy theatre, there is less
health in television, film, the arts in general and the
body politic itself. Theatre remains any society's
sharpest way to hold a live debate with itself. So it
matters.

We still complacently think that the British have the best theatre in the world. We still indeed congratulate ourselves on the power of British arts. Are they so wonderful? Well, yes – up to a point. We are a society that is still largely tolerant – a society, what is more, that takes pride in being sceptical, refusing to be awed by reputation or impressed by success. We also have a healthy suspicion of politicians. But alone among European countries, we use the word 'intellectual'as a term of abuse. And – though we are extraordinarily good at creating it – we remain by and large proudly indifferent to our arts and our artists. We are particularly indifferent to our theatre.

It is difficult to explain our apathy. Why don't we care for, and then exploit, one of our greatest resources? Our most important export is our language – rich, flexible and capable of infinite nuances. It is also capable of sending our values, our dreams and our history all round the world. This is modern colonisation; a hundred years of Hollywood have established American world trade. Hollywood is the expectation of the world. Britain could do the same

The greatest artist of all time is British: Shakespeare. He and his fellow dramatists created the richest theatrical culture in history. Yet thirty years after his death, the theatres were torn down, the actors sacked, and the dramatists sent into exile. The Puritans (the obverse side of our eccentric national creativity) had triumphed. They are triumphing now again.

Creation followed by self-righteous destruction seems to be the central need of British life. As the Second World War ended, we blessed the arts (for the first time in our history) with subsidy. The result was an explosion of talent which was historically without precedent. In the last fifty years, we have produced over twenty dramatists of world stature – more than any other country. We had long been thought of as the land without music; but our orchestras, our singers, and above all our composers (from Britten to Birtwistle) have become the envy of the world. It has been an equally extraordinary period for dance and for the visual arts.

So what do we do, faced with this golden age? We demolish the arts, or at least diminish them. The application of Thatcherite market forces have year on year reduced the resources available to the arts. Crisis management has therefore become normal management. Every arts organisation is in trouble. This book commemorates the destructive phase.

The new Labour government had a golden opportunity to revitalise our culture. For a relatively small sum of money, in national terms, the quality of our lives and our international standing could have been utterly transformed. Nothing would have such a major effect for so low a cost. But support has remained grudging and patchy. We live in towns where there is insufficient money for libraries to be opened every day of the week, but whose video stores are open twenty-four hours a day. And the arts remain in crisis.

There has been the same lack of care over our broadcasting, and this has had an immediate effect on our culture. We invented the BBC almost by accident and for seventy-five years it has entertained us, while educating us and furthering our aspirations. Now it is dumbing down in the interest of the ratings. Time was that the BBC kept commercial television honest: it had by charter, a duty to make programmes that were competitive with the BBC. Since Thatcher's deregulation, commercial television has only one duty – profit. So the BBC, now in terror that it will lose its licence, dumbs down in the interest of popularity and follows the commercial example. It dare not lag behind its competitors because it knows that politicians dare not support the difficult or the intellectual. The tabloid press would call them snobs. There was a time when more knowledge, more information and more art seemed to be gradually sharpening the perception of the population. Now market forces have reversed the trend. Taste is being cheapened.

Art and market forces never mix. Art is necessarily innovative, unexpected and frequently (particularly at its inception) unpopular. It is rare for originality to be initially commercial. Mozart's Vienna found his music too 'modern'; it took a century for him to be understood. *Waiting for Godot* was booed at its first night in 1955. Now it tops the list of the century's important plays.

To make safe and consistent money out of art, it must be dumbed down to the common denominator. Money can then be made by providing the expected stuff for the expected public. It is the principle of McDonalds taken away from catering and applied to creativity. There is a place for this, but we shouldn't confuse it with the real thing.

We now run the risk of killing originality and desensitising art. If it doesn't challenge, provoke, or illuminate, it is not fulfilling its function. On television, what is sold as infinite choice (over one hundred channels on digital television) is in fact infinitely the same. What is sold in the theatre as entertaining is bland and can easily become expected.

There is therefore an urgency about this book. The next generation will have less need of the arts: the taste will have gone. In the interests of economy, school visits to theatres and concerts have been radically reduced. There is less and less music in schools. Wherever we look, there is the same stupidity. As the Millennium approaches, we will finish building the best opera house in the world – Covent

Garden. There is insufficient money to run it. At the same time, we are building a Dome without quite knowing what to put in it. We are desperately building the cathedral without having found the God.

Radio (the cradle of many dramatists, Pinter and Stoppard among them) now has no plays longer than three-quarters-of-an-hour on its main wavelength. Audience research has told the BBC that no one will listen longer. Everywhere broadcasters and producers think about their audience's comfort rather than their provocation. So the point of art and certainly the point of theatre is being lost. Subsidy can and must restore the cutting edge.

*P*art One

The Case for Subsidy

*T*he theatre has nearly always been subsidised by somebody: the king, the court, the church, the State. The support has often been somewhat hesitant because authority never wholly trusts the theatre: it asks too many awkward questions. It is an instrument of change; it does not normally preserve the status quo. It frequently produces a live debate that frees the imagination and provokes the public to ask questions. It is therefore dangerous. All the metaphors drawn from the stage – being 'theatrical', being guilty of 'play-acting', 'being a ham' – are all pejorative. This does not apply to the other arts.

And to cover its costs, the theatre also usually needs financial help. The payer of the piper then often wonders why he does not call the tune. The questions that the theatre asks are not necessarily commercial at the time of their first performance, and paradoxically what attracts audiences finally is new questions, not old answers. So the innovative takes time to become commercial. This is basically the case for subsidy: it frees the theatre to be provocative and to fulfil its social function. It also keeps seat prices at a level where anyone who needs theatre can enjoy it. It is of course too labour-intensive and its auditoriums too small to be easily economic (actors cannot be made bigger to command bigger buildings). So the best theatre must always be free of direct market forces. Would Euripides have flourished without the support of the State? Could Shakespeare have been so consistently innovative had he not been supported by the King? 'The King's Men' was a valuable commercial name for a theatre company in Jacobean England. And it was a king who would welcome (in 1606) *King Lear* for his Christmas entertainment. In our day, would Beckett have been welcome at Buckingham Palace?

Healthy theatre is always under threat; and subsidised theatre has been dying ever since it was created. It has usually been frail, nearly always sick, and frequently on its last legs. Yet somehow it has survived because it is needed. Throughout the centuries the theatre has never completely disappeared, and, though many have lamented its passing, its ills have never proved terminal. It has a seemingly infinite capacity for rebirth. It changes its nature so that it can speak to different times and different audiences. Change is indeed often mistaken for sickness.

Change in art is always an economic risk. Literature or the visual arts can more easily risk minority audiences while they develop new means of expression. But theatre does not exist without an audience. There has to be a consensus of the public that agrees to attend the play and listen to what is being said. In order to be accessible, theatre therefore tends to be a little behind the rest of the arts — because the majority of the public is also a little behind. Perhaps this is one reason why theatre is always judged to be in decline. It is also why any new work must always break the mould if it is to be significant. The expected is the enemy of living theatre.

So we reach the first paradox: the death of the theatre usually leads to regeneration. Sometimes it is even a symptom of revolution. Monteverdi invented opera because he had to tell a story with a handful of improvising singers and musicians. Out of the need to cauterise the sentimentality of German acting, Brecht developed styles which radically changed performances and influenced productions for the whole of the second half of the twentieth century. He needed his plays to be seen clearly, without the varnish of sentiment, or the excesses of traditional German acting. So less became more, and the meaning of what was on the stage was clearer.

The Millennium gives the theatre a new aesthetic opportunity. The nineteenth century developed a stage reality so naturalistic that instead of helping the imagination, it threatened to drive it out. Rooms had their fourth wall removed, and real doors and real windows added, where before there had been painted wings and cloths. The action of a play took place in virtually actual time; and dialogue moved nearer and nearer to the simulation of ordinary speech. Gas and then electric light made darkness possible. Indeed, in Ibsen's theatre, perfectly ordinary gestures – the lighting of a lamp, or the drawing of a curtain – were revolutionary because they had not been seen on the stage before. They therefore took on a highly metaphorical significance and meant a great deal.

Yet the new naturalism brought dangers. Once theatre could actually create darkness rather than imagine it, the communication became less subtle: the audience actually couldn't see. Lady Macbeth's world of blood and darkness is best understood by hearing her words in *clear daylight*, while the actress holds a lighted candle. When the audience can see, they can hear – and they can imagine the dark. This is much more frightening than actual darkness. And the last Act of Mozart's *Figaro* (which depends on the audience knowing clearly who the disguised characters really are on this dark, Mediterranean night) only works fully in a candlelit theatre with the performers *acting* darkness, and every character clearly visible to the audience.

The new naturalism dominated theatre for over a hundred years – well into the twentieth century. It has taken the last fifty years to get free of it. We think of Chekhov and Ibsen as the high priests of this style. But even as they endorsed naturalism, they were struggling to get free of it and reach something more ambiguous and metaphorical. They knew that theatre is essentially a highly selective abstraction of reality – never reality itself.

In our time, naturalism has declined. But the theatre's potency as a place to use the imagination has consequently increased. Even fifty years ago, it was unthinkable to ask an audience to imagine a room without providing them with a room. The fourth wall was removed so that the audience could look into it; the room was correctly furnished and dressed in all its details, doors and windows and lighting were added to simulate reality. Every spotlight that supplied the artificial light had to be hidden or 'masked' from the audience. The aim was to reassure them that this was reality – not to make them *imagine* that it was.

Today, a bare stage with a table and two chairs is enough to make a room. The actors will get the audience to imagine the rest. And nobody will mind if scores of spotlights are visible above the stage. In the new century, the game of make-believe between the audience and the performer will grow stronger.

Give them some bare boards and good actors and the audience will believe that they are in Ancient Rome. Film it and the camera will show the bare boards and the good actors, but the lack of Ancient Rome will make it impossible to believe in it. The screen is literal, the theatre is metaphorical.

Here is another paradox. As the political and economic challenge to theatre grows more threatening, its power and uniqueness as a living place for the exercise of the imagination, correspondingly increases. Every day the theatre grows harder to save. And every day society needs it more desperately.

On the eve of the Millennium, the British subsidised theatre is in crisis. It faces a puritan government, which finds it too expensive, too elitist, and apparently just too *old*. The paradox is that while the young are eager to write plays and new writing has never been more vigorous, the government is indifferent to it.

The British, without doubt, are the best makers of theatre in history. If I presume to add the great Irish talents to this roll call of dramatists, its record is unmatchable. But the British abuse theatre with a casualness which often rises to hostility. They make with one hand and destroy with the other. And this they have done for centuries.

In the age of Shakespeare, the British made the greatest theatre culture ever. It was a clear demonstration of their genius for creation. But within thirty years, their genius for destruction (which is quite as pervasive) had obliterated the entire achievement. A great tradition was destroyed. Modern theatre people and scholars have therefore only the haziest idea of what an Elizabethan performance was actually like.

Perhaps it is the war in the British temperament between Cavalier eccentricity and Roundhead control which makes us subject to these puritanical fits: intense passions near to madness war with guilty restraint. Maybe this is what makes us good at theatre. It certainly makes us love it and hate it in equal measure. We seemingly cannot avoid thinking that art (and particularly performance art) is sinful and to be discouraged if not stopped. We certainly find it hard to encourage.

These neurotic swings of mood from the pragmatic to the dogmatic, from the Dionysian to the Apollonian, are particularly British. We create in pleasure and repent in pain. We destroy what we create with self-righteous enthusiasm – particularly if we feel guilty because of the joy we have found in it. We invent, but we do not conserve. So art – and particularly theatre – is something we prefer to undervalue. In this we are proud to be unlike the French. Notice that the Americans have a similar ambivalence. They are more ready to praise success than the British. They are also brilliant at making theatre; but they also take little care of it. America, after all, was founded by the Puritans.

The years since the last World War have seen the arts flourish in this country. Perhaps the greatest achievement of all was in the theatre. For the first time, Britain developed theatres with consistent policies and serious standards at the Royal Court, the Royal Shakespeare Company and the National Theatre. The responsibility to make classics live was set side by side with the performance of new plays. It was understood that no classical actor could be expert in the past unless he was thoroughly alive to the present.

British directors and designers developed to a point where their achievements at home made them welcomed abroad. And to crown all this, the British theatre could boast many playwrights – from Pinter to Hare, from Ayckbourn to Stoppard – of truly international standing. This was more, much more than any other country could field.

And the abundances continued. In 1999, there are a dozen new dramatists under thirty who are bursting with talent and energy. But unlike their seniors, they are not being helped. Regional theatres have declined because they have been consistently starved of resources: their studio theatres are mostly shut and there are fewer stages to create new plays on than there were twenty years ago. The talent is amazing, but it is not being nurtured. It has to play in improvised spaces with unpaid actors.

What encouraged this golden age in the first place? What produced it? Subsidy – subsidy that was judiciously applied to keep seat prices low (and thus develop the next generation of audiences); subsidy used to encourage and promote new talent.

Subsidy has been supplied by the Arts Council – a body invented after the war by Maynard Keynes, the great economist. He wanted to protect the arts as well as encourage them. Government was to be kept at arm's length, although government supplied the money. It was the Arts Council, made up of major artists, who set the standards and encouraged creativity. Art was not planned into existence. But once there, it was encouraged by subsidy.

The Arts Council had its moments of absurdity. But its freedom from political interference and its record of creativity made it the envy of the world. It has been destroyed. Margaret Thatcher did not believe in subsidising the arts: she thought it distorted the market and probably encouraged Leftist tendencies. She was unimpressed by the huge achievements of subsidy when she came to power in 1979; and those of us who worked in the arts were quickly made to feel unnecessary – almost encouraged to go and look for a proper job. We were certainly told that the good times were over. And they were. From the Chairmanship of William Rees-Mogg, the Arts Council was gradually dismantled and became not a representative body defending the arts, but a government office diminishing them.

Unfortunately, the inability to accept minority art or minority thinking has been a characteristic of both political parties in the media age. They are frightened of high standards. Market forces must destroy the original and disregard the unique. So if they are applied to the school curriculum (which the Conservatives did) we must end up with airport fiction rather than Shakespeare.

The Conservatives didn't quite find the courage to stop subsidy for the arts. Instead, they subtly undermined and discredited it. Arts organisations have been systematically starved for twenty years, usually by making sure that any increase was always less than inflation.

Private sponsorship was introduced in 1979. The argument sounded credible: we were a mixed economy, and therefore private enterprise should be encouraged to support new developments in the arts. But we were promised that sponsorship would never be allowed to replace basic government funding. Subsidy was to continue to pay for the primary purpose of all arts organisations.

The promise was broken. Year on year, through Thatcher's time and then Major's, subsidy to the arts was pegged annually below inflation. This was a way of reducing subsidy without the public noticing it. Year on year, more and more sponsorship money was needed in order just to stand still. Soon theatres were spending as much on sponsorship departments as they were on productions. It was the only way to survive. And bureaucracy thrived. Soon a safe career in the arts meant being a consultant or an assessor to the Arts Council.

The performing arts were also told to charge whatever the market would bear for their tickets. The primary purpose of subsidy was thus quietly undermined. It had originally been designed to keep prices low enough to make tickets readily available. Now art became more and more elitist, because it was more and more expensive. It was thus soon easier to attack it for being subsidised.

There followed years of increasing muddle, produced by chronic underfunding. The golden age was speedily tarnished, standards declined, and management became more hit and miss. Every arts organisation in the country has been, or is, in severe crisis. And crisis management speedily makes for bad management. And in the case of the Royal Opera House, government pressures created an indefensible 'toffs'' opera which regularly charged £200 a ticket, while drawing a subsidy of £15,000,000 a year from the taxpayer. No wonder it was unpopular.

The policies of past governments have forced Covent Garden into its present absurd position. How can anyone be expected to manage with insufficient resources? A gleeful media (that by and large hates the arts because it enjoys playing boisterously to the art-hating majority) jumped up and down on the corpse. Covent Garden has actually produced some of the world's best opera in the last fifty years. Are we proud of this? Apparently not.

It is now entirely possible that the Labour government (very sensitive to any charge of elitism) may well be the instrument to destroy our operatic culture. Perhaps they will dare to do what the Conservatives hadn't quite the courage to attempt. Or they will have to find a great deal more money and disguise the fact so as to save their faces.

Faced with the mess created by twenty years of Tory indifference to the arts, New Labour has swept in and called for more and more management. Businessmen have accordingly been appointed to the Chairmanship of the Arts Council and the Royal Opera House. Rationalisations are proceeding apace. This is a serious misreading of the situation. What the arts all over the country need is not more management, but a realistic and constant level of funding. The arts have been attacked and jeered at for years: some steady and consistent support would work wonders. It is not just money but confidence that needs to be restored.

New Labour arrived with promises from Tony Blair that creativity in the new society would be cherished and honoured. Every arts organisation in the country felt hopeful. Each and every one of them had endured years of shrinking resources under Thatcher, while being expected to provide the same output to the same standard. This had produced a great deal of demoralisation.

The hopes were soon dashed. To the dismay of the arts community, the first visible gesture that New Labour made towards the arts was to cut in 1997 the Arts Council appropriation by £3,000,000. In terms of the nation's economy, it was a meaningless sum; but it wrecked a number of small theatres and dance companies. What was the point? Presumably the government wanted to send a message that the arts did not figure on their list of priorities. Was the new government reassuring middle-England that they were not going to be soft on the arts, in spite of what had been said before the election?

In 1998, more money was made available, but it was patchily applied and as far as the theatre was concerned, the only discernible policy was a negative one. During the season 1998/99, 55% of regional theatres were on standstill grants. Many of them were thought unlikely to survive the year. All of them felt that they were irrelevancies about to be sacrificed so that the large theatres could live on. All this was accompanied by a chorus of enthusiastic government poodles, led by Melvyn Bragg, telling us that the arts were being better funded. Tell that to the actor on the dole or the dancer not allowed to dance.

We have a civilised, articulate and reasonable Arts Minister in Chris Smith. He consistently makes all the right noises. He knows why money has to be given to the arts: it will ensure that art is available to all. But he is given insufficient money and insufficient power. The gap (so pervasive with New Labour) between what is said to be happening and what is really happening is evident for everyone to see.

The policy for the theatre seems to be a confusing blend of management and feasibility studies (which have cost a great deal of money), with attempted reformation by supporting the big boys and letting the little ones die. All of this adds up at the beginning of 1999 to a pattern of indifferent destruction.

The philistinism of New Labour is very worrying. The visible, the trendy – pop music, design, video, film, architecture – are the creative happenings that seem to interest them. They seem not have realised that, unless dance, music and art are encouraged in primary schools (they are, after all, the most primitive forms of *knowing*), not only will there be no audiences in the future, but the talent to develop and execute the new and sometimes profitable arts will not be there either. Research and training are the province of the old arts that need subsidy; primarily, they are the performing arts. Unless it supports them, the government will find that its much vaunted 'creative industries' do not have the right level of talent to make them work.

It is all a considerable puzzle. Why should a government that says it is dedicated to education be indifferent to the arts? With the decline of religion, art becomes crucial to the health of a democracy. It helps society understand why it lives and how it lives. So why not encourage it? The present government's mistakes are not just of passing interest, not just a disappointment because they promised so much. Nothing could enrich our children, our international standing, and our ability to govern ourselves so much as an enlightened patronage of the arts. What we are getting instead is something which will, I am sure, be seen in the great tradition of English puritanism – narrow-minded and joyless at the worst, and indifferent to excellence at the best.

As we go into the new century, one question needs asking and asking urgently. Do we want the arts or don't we? If we do want them, we should be prepared to pay for them, just as we are prepared to pay for education or for hospitals or for defence. If we don't want them, we should stop subsidy. We should stop compromising and causing misery to many thousands of people who try to work in the arts.

They are, by and large, a hard working and underpaid lot. They don't want bigger and bigger handouts. They dream of the day when the country gives them sufficient resources to provide reasonably priced art to every man woman and child who has a taste for it.

I suppose any politician would say that governments don't care about the arts because generally speaking the public don't. Both political parties are very supportive of the arts when they are in opposition because they can make minor political contests out of them. But they don't care about them when they are in power. The public indeed only react when the arts are removed, and specifically when the arts are no longer available for their children. So providing that a theatre survives, even if it is underfunded, struggling and miserable, the public remains generally apathetic to its difficulties.

It is a human fault not to defend our basic rights. Freedom of speech, for instance, requires constant protection; all governments hide information if they can get away with it. Basic care and basic education is the right of every individual. So are the arts. But we take all this for granted and protect our strengths.

For fifty years, even with all the struggles, we have had subsidised art and regulated television. If the public soon find themselves living in a land without symphony orchestras, art galleries, or theatres — a land dominated by imported television, with art which is bland, unexceptional and multi-national, they will realise what they have lost. The electorate should reflect on that before they decide that subsidy is as out-dated as the old BBC. Otherwise they will be left with a few palaces of culture – a National Theatre in London and a great concert hall in Birmingham. But the small centres that produce tomorrow's talent, and most of all, tomorrow's audience, will be gone.

There are other reasons for subsidy. Higher living standards inevitably mean higher wages, and this means that a labour-intensive activity like a theatre company or a symphony orchestra – which performs for you and for your fellow audience members only on this single night – becomes more and more expensive. There cannot be more seats because the experience has to remain on a human scale. Theatre and concerts are uniquely made each evening for a minority; the experience is destroyed if it is mass-produced. And anything that is not mass-produced in our society is getting more expensive.

The economy of the theatre has changed in our century because standards and expectations have also changed – usually for the better. Regional theatres know that they cannot now have a provincial standard that is less than the metropolitan one. Young actors can no longer go to the regions to 'learn' their jobs. Television means that the public expects actors as experienced at their local rep as they are at the National Theatre. This is excellent, but costs money. Over the last twenty years, many British regional theatres have closed or have had to reduce their output. As the amount of drama shrinks, the importance of the two major companies – the National Theatre and the Royal Shakespeare Company – becomes greater. Without them (and how very nearly we didn't get either) our theatre would now be in a sorry state. Not only do they train tomorrow's technicians, actors, dramatists and directors; they develop tomorrow's audiences. The habit of going to the theatre is made and sustained by having a theatre to go to.

We might easily be in the same impoverished state as the New York theatre. Each season there may see a new sensation – the new musical or the new dramatist. But where can the young theatregoer find first-class Shakespeare, Ibsen, Chekhov, Shaw or Beckett? There may be one good classical production at the Lincoln Center; there may be a new voice off-Broadway. But the central library of classics is not available. As a consequence, the theatrical experience of New York is hardly rich enough to reinvent itself. Innovation needs tradition to support it.

In Britain we can happily add the Royal Court Theatre to our two flagships, so the classics are constantly confronted by new writing. Ever since George

Devine took it over in 1956 it has, each decade, found the next generation of playwrights. It has always had unyielding standards and the courage to take risks. Its detractors have derided it for being a ghetto, but this has been its strength. Minorities are always the initial support of any new talent. And from John Osborne to Sarah Kane, the talent has always come to the Royal Court. While we have a theatre building dedicated to new writing, there will always be new writing.

There are only three theatres in Britain that have the resources to work consistently and seriously — and this does not mean luxuriously. They have rehearsal and technical conditions to a standard that would be regarded as automatic on the Continent. They are the result of subsidy. Neither the National Theatre, the Royal Shakespeare Company, nor the Royal Court can pay the people who work for them properly. Nor are their seat prices now low enough for them to fulfil their social responsibilities. But at least their resources make sure their work is well executed.

Yet to provide these minimal conditions, both the large, classical theatres have been forced to become too big. I know, because I watched them grow and nursed them both. For twenty-five years of my life I have lived the subsidised theatre. I created the Royal Shakespeare Company in 1960, and after ten years running it, spent another fifteen years with the National Theatre – a time when I was responsible for moving it into its new South Bank buildings. Each company had to do more and more each year, because productivity and size was the only way to justify the subsidy. They have both grown bigger and bigger in order to preserve proper working conditions.

Some years after I left, the Royal Shakespeare Company announced a record number of first nights in one year. It was forty-three. I was appalled. How could so much work be particular?

The National Theatre, with its three theatres, its tours, and its remit to do a spectrum of world drama from Aeschylus to David Hare and beyond, has the same problem. Both organisations are gargantuan. It is very difficult to make an aesthetic out of such a vast programme. It is even more difficult to make a theatre company which, if human contact is to be maintained, cannot be more than thirty or forty people. But if either organisation does fewer productions, its subsidy will assuredly be reduced and its potency decline. And the first thing that will suffer is the working conditions. So both companies have to accept diversity and become like Harrods – retailers rather than instigators: department stores of fine theatre.

Both organisations have also suffered from the growth of bureaucracy – a disease which has already afflicted the BBC and the universities. When a financial crisis appears, what is easily removable is removed. In the theatre this means: cut the productions and cut the number of actors. The bureaucrats always remain: they are the sitting tenants that are drawing up the plans for the cuts. With all this pressure, neither of the two big companies can easily have a visible aesthetic: their output is too complex and their vision necessarily too broad. So the Royal Shakespeare announces that it will be doing less Shakespeare in order to attract more audiences. The National continues to do commercial musicals in order to diminish its deficit. I have nothing against musicals: a few of them are very fine. But I don't believe that campaigns were fought for one-hundred-and-fifty years to build a national theatre so that we could have straight runs of American musicals in the main house, while *King Lear* has to be confined to the Cottesloe. I know well the reasons for this: they are economic – and finally political. Blame the governments rather than those running the theatre.

Some fifteen years ago, I presented *Guys and Dolls* and Aeschylus' *Oresteia* in repertory in the Olivier theatre. I thought the mix of the two showed the breadth of the National Theatre's repertory. In fact I was roundly condemned in the press for having such a small repertory – some commentators even thought that the National Theatre should not be doing *Guys and Dolls* at all. Times change. Now a straight run of a single play is accepted as a necessary evil. Economics rule.

The decline in subsidy has had the biggest effect on the regional theatres. They have been starved even more than theatres in London. Wages have plummeted, and standards have dropped. Young directors see no reason to go and run a regional theatre. They earn a miserable salary, and they are given equally miserable resources. Proper work is hardly possible. Some twenty years ago, the Bristol Old Vic had a thriving studio. In it, the assistant to the director was doing a series of extraordinary classical productions. His name was Adrian Noble. He is now director of the Royal Shakespeare Company. Today, the studio is mostly shut, and the director of the Bristol Old Vic cannot afford an assistant. Where are tomorrow's directors to develop their craft? The existence of many diverse theatres means that many diverse talents can surprise us. New artists can develop and new audiences. And if the theatre as a whole is to reach its full potential, the regional theatres must thrive. Only then can we talk about a truly national audience.

Fringe theatre, playing in small and unlikely places, happens all over the country. It is fitful, but then it should be. Wonderful things occur alongside terrible things. But the vitality exists because of the support of the actors. They are the subsidy. They often put up with the humiliation of working for no money – or just for bus fares, because they believe. The majority of Fringe theatres in London are staffed by virtually unpaid people.

Not that there is much money to be made in the theatre today, even by established stars. There was a short period in the late Sixties when the National Theatre and the Royal Shakespeare Company paid wages, that, while they were not commercial, were at least possible to live on; an actor could maintain his family. With years and years of financial stringency, that time has long gone. Actors now work at our two major subsidised theatres because they endorse the necessity of doing the work, but for small money. They are in a very real sense subsidising them. They work for a fifth or sixth of their commercial rate because they believe in what is being done.

This now applies everywhere. Actors earn their living through television or voice-overs, and they can occasionally indulge their passion for the theatre. They can extend their talent, stretch their abilities, and be immediately judged by a live response. If this idealism ever leaves the profession (as it has in America), the theatre will be quickly diminished. Most American agents do not even bother to return a call enquiring for an actor to work on the stage. There is no money in it, and it is not worth the client's considerable risk. But here, the British actor still defends the theatre. Does the British public realise that our theatre, which feeds our television, stimulates and educates our children, and provides the entire country with plane loads of tourists every year, is actually subsidised by the dedication of its actors?

Generally, the British support institutions, not individuals. There is a mass of dramatic talent in this country which is not being cared for, and much of it goes to waste. A very small increase in resources would result in a huge explosion of activity. Theatre is made by people, not by buildings. To people in Britain's hard-pressed theatres, it must be tempting to see in Europe colleagues who are allowed to make good work in good conditions. Here, every theatre is wondering if the next grant will be maintained, or simply whether it dare start planning next year's season.

Alan Ayckbourn's extraordinary achievement in Scarborough proves the innate strength of a properly run regional theatre. Britain could easily support ten Scarboroughs up and down the country if there was real encouragement coming from the government. That is not to say that we would find ten more Ayckbourns. But we could easily find ten people who, if not geniuses, can still enable good theatre to be created. They might be actors, writers or directors. They are not hard to find.

By the seventies, it seemed that the case for subsidy had been won for all time. Then came Thatcherism and the gradual decay of the arts. Now subsidy is seen as a 'handout' and a proper debate among artists about resources as 'whingeing for a handout'. Unless we understand the need for subsidy, our arts will not flourish. And if our arts diminish, our society will become dumber, more brutish, and less creative. It will not only aspire less, but build less. Will the public shrug off the loss of the golden age and decide that it was just a happy chance and not worth fighting for? Or will they make the government understand that they want their theatres, their concert halls and their art galleries for the sake of their children? Everything in the arts inter-acts. Kill the theatre and the talent available to television and films will diminish. Cut training in the visual arts and our national ability to design will be crippled. Stop teaching music in schools, and our lucrative pop industry will become less profitable. There is an urgent need to understand the threat to our culture.

Part Two
The Case
for a Company

Creative work in a theatre has always been done by a company. Here is another paradox. A company does the best work – but good work can also create a company. It may form itself by chance because a collection of actors in a commercial production have worked often together in the past. Or it may be stimulated by the playwright's demands or the director's inspiration. It can happen in a matter of days. But the potent theatre company takes longer to develop, as actors grow together, learning each others' working habits, learning, indeed how they dislike as much as how they like each other. Making theatre needs everyone to accept that they are dependent on everyone else. The messenger with one line can ruin the leading actor's scene if he does not speak at the right tempo and in the right mood. The wig-mistress who is late for a quick-change can wreck the concentration of everyone on stage. Company work recognises dependency. Indeed, it celebrates it. It is less necessary in opera, where the dependency of the singer is more often focused on the conductor and orchestra than on his colleagues. And the dependency is not necessarily a need in filming, where the relationship of the actor to the camera is more important than the relationship with his fellow actor.

A good theatre company is small – some thirty to forty people; a hundred, if you add all the technicians and front-of-house staff. This is the size of a healthy tribe. Everyone can know everyone else. A good rehearsal with a creative company can feel like a metaphor for a healthy family, or an ideal society. The work is done well because the interchange is candid and free.

A good performance also needs this company spirit. A production cannot be re-created each night without the agreement, co-operation and care of every member of the company, on stage and off. It is a genuine consensus.

I did a year's work at the Old Vic in London 1997, thanks to the generosity of David Mirvish. I wrote down many of the practices which had angered me during my twenty-five years at the National and the RSC and resolved not to repeat them. What follows is therefore about practice, not theory. In a sense, the organisation I made *was* the aesthetic. What I tried to do at the Old Vic is offered here as evidence for a debate: an attempt to break the mould as we enter the twenty-first century.

At the Old Vic with our small company of twenty-five actors we found that the audiences' traditional responses were still strong: they loved seeing the same actors in different parts; they had an enthusiasm for seeing young talent develop; a feeling that the group had a strong and intimate relationship with it which was growing with every production. The more cohesive the company became, the more it felt capable of an immediate dialogue with its audience, and the more it felt able to arouse an imaginative response. This is the true process of live theatre.

At the Old Vic, we quickly created a supportive audience who were making regular visits at very cheap prices. Our low-cost ticket scheme meant that five plays could be seen for £10 each. So there was a continuing audience with a developing dialogue between those who watched and those who played. This is not fanciful. It was a feeling that became more palpable as the season went on.

A theatre company has the same belief in itself as a good orchestra or a good string quartet. It trusts in the potency and strength of its productions. This pride in itself directly effects the experience of each performance and the attitude of the audience. A proud company plays to half-full house: a confused company plays to a half-empty one.

Company work makes an actor's life richer. The big part one night is followed by the small part the next. The small part is often richly played by a leading actor who would not normally undertake such a role. Typecasting is avoided. In the commercial world the obvious characteristics of an actor are emphasised so that he plays regularly the same kind of part. More improbable and dangerous casting is always better, because it reflects the unexpectedness of life. In a company, the actor can take risks. So can the director as he casts.

In this television age, the theatre has once more become a place of imagination, freed of naturalism and of unnecessary decoration. At the Old Vic, we therefore tried to seize the moment aesthetically. John Gunter developed a simple design where the actor and his text was clearly presented on a well-planked stage. The actor, his passion, a few visual elements and some bare boards: this was all we had or needed. The audience's imagination was encouraged – we had no technology or complication. This not only gave the stage back to the actor; it once more made the dramatist pre-eminent. With the right text and the right actors, the bare boards became anywhere.

By having a strong design discipline at the Old Vic – in effect a permanent stage – we spent little of our money on building and rebuilding sets. Our

changeovers from one play to another took one hour –
no more than is customary to set back to the
beginning of a single play. We were able to play real
repertory – which meant a change of play after every
performance. Lear no longer had to play the part
twice in one day. This constantly changing programme gave variety and stimulation to the actor and
choice to the audience. It also meant, noticeably, that
every production grew better and livelier rather than
shrivelling. The repeated performances of the theatre
can lead to monotony, to formulas, and finally to
completely dead occasions. In repertory, every performance is an event. The play always finds new life.

Because of the size of the sets, the repertory
system at the National Theatre and the Royal Shakespeare Company has often to be governed entirely by
technical considerations. It costs a fortune to tear a
set down on Monday only to put it up again on
Wednesday. It is therefore sensible to give each play
three or four consecutive performances. This is not
repertory. Unfortunately, when several plays are in
performance, each one can disappear for a fortnight
or more. And when a new production is added, the
rest of the plays have to drop out for a week or even
longer. The actors return in a maelstrom of nerves
after the gap and have to be given a word rehearsal.
But if the actor plays one part on Monday, another
on Tuesday, and returns again to his original part on

Wednesday, security can be enjoyed as well as freshness.

Did the permanent stage at the Old Vic result in monotony? I don't think so. There were no complaints from the critics or from the public, and several other designers enjoyed using John Gunter's stage as an environment in which they could place the essential images for their own play. Everything on the stage was strictly demanded by the action, and at all times we tried to avoid decoration.

We never needed to go 'dark' in order to dress-rehearse a new play, because the ready availability of the stage allowed us to dress-rehearse during the day. We then maintained our repertory each evening. The maximum use of the stage was therefore enjoyed both for rehearsals and for performances. And for seven days a week, the theatre was alive.

This discipline meant that the stage could be given back to the actors. The outside world erroneously believes that actors rehearse on stages. They don't. Stages are usually filled with other scenery that makes an inappropriate stage area for the play that is being rehearsed, or they are filled with stage-staff taking down or putting up a set, or bands of electricians pushing large ladders around. The last person who can normally get on to the stage is the actor.

Productions are created in rehearsal rooms. They are usually cold or hot or dark or blindingly light or dusty or noisy – conditions that make it almost impossible to do the sensitive work needed to create a play. Theatre people put up with bad rehearsal conditions because, as usual, they make the best of it. Then, at the very moment when the actors are at their most vulnerable, when their performance is just coming to life, they find themselves on a stage and in an unfamiliar space. They are buttoned into their costumes and told to be free and relaxed. Actors endure this traumatic experience with every play.

No play should be designed and no costume conceived in the abstract. Unfortunately, because of economic considerations, most sets are designed well before rehearsals begin, and most actors are confronted on the first day of rehearsal with a finished costume design. They are told that this is how they are to look.

Such work is neither organic nor creative. One of the director's jobs is to help a designer collaborate with the actors so that the play can be given physical life. This can only be done by painstaking work. Economic considerations mean that mostly, this cannot happen. The actor is often told about the designs when they are already executed. Often he feels that he is already in a revival. And he is not as good as the original cast.

One of my best experiences was when I directed *Antony and Cleopatra* with Judi Dench, Anthony

Hopkins and Michael Bryant at the National Theatre. We had twelve weeks to rehearse. We began with no designs, and for the first six weeks Alison Chitty sat sketching as we analysed the problems of each scene and each character. At the end of six weeks, she was ready to design. The work was therefore truly organic.

There was a similar way of working at the Old Vic. Because the stage belonged to our actors, we rehearsed there a great deal of the time. Design could be left late, because it was minimal. We did our technical work and our lighting during the last two weeks of rehearsals – while the actors were still working on the stage. There were no agonising technical marathons, with sixteen-hour days which leave the actor exhausted as he approaches his first meeting with the public.

None of this was backstage luxury. It made our efforts noticeably better, and we all recognised that this was the way we always ought to work. The actors grew together as a company, and the technicians joined in also.

Theatres must play seven days a week in the future. Theatre buildings spend too much of their time dark and empty. At the Old Vic, I found the most extraordinary public response on Sundays. By playing at three o'clock and eight o'clock, we showed that there is a vast London audience for Sunday theatre.

Sunday afternoon is an ideal time for a family to go to the theatre together, so that was when we offered classics and well-known plays. On Sunday evenings, we did new plays, and had the support of the young, predominantly cinema-going audience. Each Friday, I looked at the coming Sunday evening's box-office return and worried: there were so few bookings. But on Sunday night, there was always a long queue of young people waiting to buy tickets. We always started late as a consequence. The young do not like to book and refuse to develop the habit. They go to the theatre as they go to the cinema – on impulse. This is a lesson that managements have to learn for the future.

And the entertainment industry generally has to understand the crucial importance of Sundays. It could easily become the best theatre day of the week. For years, musicians in orchestras have not expected to be paid more if they play on Sunday. They have had other days off instead. The same must happen to the theatre, if it is to survive. For fifteen years, I watched the South Bank thriving on a Sunday, with the Queen Elizabeth Hall, The Hayward Gallery, The Purcell Room, and The Royal Festival Hall all thronged with people. Next door, the three auditoriums of the National Theatre were locked and barred. Because of special Sunday rates of pay, the cost of opening them was too high.

At the Old Vic, we mixed classics with new plays and classical techniques with modern sensibility. It made for extraordinary energy. Ever since I created the Royal Shakespeare Company, I have believed that the division between classics and contemporary writing is false. No classic is worth reviving unless it is contemporary in the sense that it speaks directly to the modern audience. The lessons of the past give us something to think about in the present. But unless the play's preoccupations are vivid and contemporary, a revival of it is of purely academic interest. Audiences likewise love new plays. They want to hear what their writers have to say about now. And working on new plays helps to inform and enliven a company's appoach to the classics.

At the Old Vic, we did new plays on Sundays and Mondays. Each play was only given initially for eight performances: the risk was little and the budget was tiny. By the end of the 1997 season, we had mounted thirteen productions for just over £300,000. That figure would buy only one and a half – or possibly two – small productions in the West End. So our aesthetic had brought us not only flexibility, but low costs. None of it would have been possible without a company.

In this century, the theatre has become more and more a collective activity. Nonetheless there is always a leader – an editor whose decision is endorsed by the group as final. The emergence of this leader seems to be almost automatic. If the nominated director is not actually fulfilling his function properly, one of the actors or the playwright may quietly or unquietly subvert him. The new leader becomes the one that every actor appeals to for guidance.

Making theatre without a director is finally impossible because the group needs an outside eye. This may be the dramatist or it may be the leading actor; sometimes it is the management. But the company demands to be lead.

I have run theatres for virtually all my life, and consequently I have had the privilege of watching nearly all the great theatre directors at work – from Bergman to Zeffirelli and Visconti; or from Brook to Guthrie and Nunn.

And here is another paradox. I have seen great directors talk palpable nonsense to a group of actors and get wonderful results. I have seen second-class directors talk brilliantly and get nowhere at all.

What is this mystery? The great director (like the great conductor) has a visceral ability to communicate beyond words and beyond thoughts. It is dangerous territory. As an actor once said to me, 'Brilliant bullshit can often produce gold'.

The quality remains, though, inexplicable. Years ago, I was directing *Tristan und Isolde* at Covent Garden. George Solti was conducting. He listened to about fifteen minutes of the orchestra, standing in the auditorium. The conductor was his assistant. The tempi were Solti's – they had been established during the painstaking rehearsals. Solti listened gravely and attentively. He then went down to the podium and conducted the same section. He did not say a word to the orchestra by way of correction or inspiration; the tempi were the same – but the whole performance was transformed. Were the orchestra not bothering for the assistant? I don't think so. They were galvanised into expressing the music by something beyond words that was emanating from Solti. A director can have the same effect.

The director's function is to be part friend, part instructor, part doctor, part lover, part educator, part editor, part technician, part analyst. He must like actors and be as open in rehearsal to them as they are to him. A good rehearsal depends on total physical relaxation in the director. However much the director may know of the play or where he wishes to guide his actors, it is the spontaneous work done on the hoof which is creative. It comes, of course, from a thorough knowledge of the text; but how that text is expressed is always a matter of spontaneous group creation. The director was a late nineteenth-century invention. With the complex ensembles of Chekhov and Ibsen, and the increasingly elaborate technology of stage lighting and sound, the necessity for one person to co-ordinate all these elements became crucial. Stanislavsky was clearly a dictator. Yet he set his actors in an environment which was so alive that they drew strength from it. He was the first great director.

Harley Granville Barker, the first great English director, was meticulous but similarly authoritarian. He demanded more analysis than his contemporary, Bernard Shaw. Shaw's rehearsal methods were to give the moves and then repeat the scene time after time, giving copious notes after each run-through. Actors were not allowed to stop within a scene, or to comment until Shaw had spoken.

I have seen working methods change radically in my lifetime. Tyrone Guthrie made his rehearsals like a great prep-school party – and he was the authoritative schoolmaster giving the pupils a good time. Michel St Denis, great teacher and great inspirer, was by today's standard extremely dogmatic in his demands. He gave the actor the result: it was the actor's job to find out how to motivate it.

My generation, led by Peter Brook, have striven to be less dogmatic and more flexible. We were the first group of directors who dared to say to the actor: 'I don't know: let us find out'. This is still a dangerous thing to say in the German theatre. They fear that a man who admits doubts may not be capable of being their leader. In Germany, a director must always pretend to know the answer.

Theatre should never be made from pre-arranged plans. The director and the actors need all the understanding of the text they can bring to the rehearsal room; but then the organic process of questioning must begin. Led by the director, the actors make a journey to find out how to express this particular play at this particular time to this particular audience. It requires technique and experiment, experience and trust. It is a discovery – not an imposition of results. This is how my generation rehearses. The work is open and democratic, until the moment (late on in rehearsals) when the director has to become the editor and decide what, of all the riches that have been created, should be used. Even then, there must be a consensus between actors and director about how a scene shall be played. This agreement is vital because each night the actors meet to recreate the scene in a particular way, with an agreed atmosphere and agreed moves. They make it live again. It is still a miracle to me that a well-rehearsed production can vary in time by as little as thirty seconds from one evening to the next. This means that the consensus is strong, that the bonding inside the company is strong. A bad production by an ill-formed company will vary in time much more.

As we move into the next century, rehearsal methods will doubtless change again. But work based on collaboration and consensus, given the increasingly democratic societies that we live in, must surely make a return to autocratic ways impossible. The company will remain pre-eminent.

Great theatres have never been created by administrators, and I think it is unlikely that they will ever be. Artists are generally good managers: they have to be. They understand priorities and the keeping to deadlines rather better, in my experience, than many businessmen. Good art can only be good if it comes out of meticulous obsession and organisation.

Fifty years ago, the theatre had a great prejudice against the intellectual. There was a feeling that playing the play had very little to do with intellectual discipline or scholarship. Those days, mercifully, are over.

Theatre people and academics now often talk the same language. They both, of course have their extreme positions. Concept theatre, (where the director of a Shakespeare play, for example, tells the actors what the production is to say before they have examined what the play says) is as uncreative as the deconstructions of minor Shakespearean scholarship. They both contrive to destroy the marvel of Shakespeare, denigrate his particularity, and forget that his plays were made to be performed. Above all, they are ambiguous and contradictory.

I believe in verbal theatre. On my stage, the beginning is the word. That is not to say that physical theatre – mime and dance – cannot be very expressive. But nothing for me can match the complexity and ambiguity of action defined by words, or silence created by speech, or of a great antithetical paradox by Shakespeare. In the theatre, the word focuses. Unless the actor defines them by word, complexities and ambiguities hardly exist in the theatre. The words define Pinter's eloquent pauses; they express the life-enhancing despair of Beckett; or the lyricism of Tennessee Williams, as his dependent clauses surge on and on.

These men are thought to write naturalistic dialogue. But of course they don't – just as Chekhov or Ibsen didn't. They are all poetic dramatists with very precise styles and very individual voices. They simulate real speech, but for the actor to try to make Pinter more 'real' by ignoring his punctuation, or Tennessee Williams more colloquial by splitting up his long sentences into Method-driven fragments, simply ruins the resonance of the writing. It is not easy to play any of these great dramatists. They all have a particular voice. Bernard Shaw's sentences need pursuing to the very end. It is a disaster to play his semi-colons as full-stops. For his rhetoric to operate, even his full stops often need to be treated as commas. Then the energy is released.

These are technical matters – and a company has the opportunity to study them and develop a uniform approach to particular dramatists. The actor should only breathe in Shakespeare on the end of a line – never, never on the caesura, or he will split the blank-verse line. His job is to preserve the sanctity of the line, the form, the balance of it. And the excitement – like great jazz playing – is how nearly the regularity of the line is destroyed while still being preserved. The humanity of Shakespeare is expressed by his irregularities, just as Mozart's sense of anguish is conveyed by his amazing chromaticism. They both inherited a rigid form that they could make flexible and irregular. By such means, they expressed their humanity.

And here is another paradox for the new century. In music, the modern obsession is to find the purest, earliest ur-text. Original instruments – or at least original methods of playing – are sought so that Mozart may be *cleaned*, as an ancient painting is cleaned. Everything is done in the name of authenticity. Cuts are restored. What is sacred is the composer's original thought.

In the theatre, it is quite different. Music critics would go mad if a few bars of Mozart or Wagner were cut here and there. But great chunks of Shakespeare are ripped out of the plays without the drama critics apparently even noticing. Or if they notice they are largely indifferent. Who really needs the first scene of *Hamlet* anyway? It seems much more original to delete it. In the theatre, directors cut because something does not work, or often because they don't know how to make it work. To cut because the text has lost all meaning seems to me permissible. To cut and edit in order to give Shakespeare a new slant seems hubris of the worst kind. Having had some experience of how rightly protective Samuel Beckett and Harold Pinter are of their texts, I wonder what Shakespeare would say if he saw the delicate rhythms of *Twelfth Night* ruined by a director who decided to put the second scene first. It has been done. It has even been said to be more logical.

I wonder if Shakespeare will still be current in two hundred years? Will he, indeed, be comprehensible? The inevitable alteration in our vocabulary means that he becomes more and more difficult to understand. I am glad that I have lived at a time when an actor delivering a speech with intelligence can make an audience understand collectively what they would not immediately understand individually. This direct communication remains one of the wonders of live theatre. Shakespeare tells the actor when to pause, when to come in on cue, when to go fast, when to go slow, and which words to accent. He does not tell the actor *why* he should do any of these things, but his writing is as precise as a page of music. Providing you can read them, all the dynamics are there. I was taught the text of Shakespeare by George

Rylands of the Marlowe Society. This Cambridge university group was founded at the turn of the century, inspired by the example of William Poel, the great scourge of Irving. Poel brought Shakespeare back to Hamlet's requirements, speaking it 'trippingly on the tongue'. His rapid technique was learnt from the older actors in Macready's company. They had been taught by Kean who had been taught by Garrick who had been taught by Betterton. That was as far back as he could go. There the tradition ends. The Puritans destroyed it.

William Poel taught Harley Granville Barker. He also directed, as Cressida, the seventeen-year-old Edith Evans, fresh from her milliner's shop. She was one of the first great actors I worked with as a young director. Evening after evening, I begged her to tell me the rules of verse that Poel had taught to her. They were the same as George Rylands had taught to me. The Marlowe Society had been founded on Poel's beliefs by Rupert Brooke and his contemporaries in 1903.

These traditions matter. And they are the life-blood of a theatre company. They keep Shakespeare alive. Laurence Olivier's verse speaking was not the same as Sybil Thorndike's; Richard Burton's was not the same as Olivier's; and Judi Dench's is not the same as Paul Scofield's. But the differences are differences of personal emphasis, not of organic structure.

Fashion may change, but the centre holds. There are now only some forty or fifty actors in Britain who can speak blank verse, and some four or five directors who can orchestrate it. The tradition is threatened unless the profession does something to uphold it.

It is too early yet to say what the new Globe Theatre, Sam Wanamaker's wonderful dream, will bring to our understanding of Shakespeare. At last we have an Elizabethan daylight stage. I believe it is not accurate in many respects, but it can still give us a vivid sense of the articulation of a Shakespearean play. This is also the obvious place for a company to attempt a rigorous study of Shakespeare's verse and speaking techniques. In time, the actors will find themselves impelled to adopt them. If Shakespeare is not spoken correctly, the audience cannot understand him. Conditions out of doors will make the adoption of necessary techniques inescapable. Once again, the creation of a company, all working the same way, will be mandatory.

What kind of stage shall we have for the theatre of the next millennium? A theatre led by imagination and freed of literalism? Or a computer-driven miracle of lasers and illusions? The theatre has moved out of the picture-frame in the last hundred years. The rhythms of Appia and Gordon Craig, and the textures revealed by the use of spotlights, have turned the magic-lantern pictures of the gas-lit

Victorian theatre into the stark sculptures of modern design.

As the picture frame was progressively discarded, the stage itself projected further and further forward until it was once more creating the intimacy of the Regency theatre or the epic naturalism of the Elizabethan stage. Tyrone Guthrie's experiment at Stratford, Ontario, with a thrust stage (reproduced in Britain at Chichester, though somewhat inadequately because the auditorium is not high enough) is all part of the same impulse – a need which has been at the centre of Peter Brook's experiments with audiences. Everyone has wanted to make the performer and the audience inhabit *one* space, not two. The interaction of audience on performer and performer on audience thus becomes greater. The space becomes one and the actor can shout or whisper, speak quietly or orate. Everywhere theatre people have striven for the same thing – an intimate, yet epic space. A Shakespearean space.

If performers arrive in a town square and an audience gathers, they place themselves in a natural confrontational relationship. The audience does not watch the performer in the round or in the half round. It certainly does not watch (if it can help it) from the sides. For an actor to command an audience, he must be able to see every member of it with his peripheral vision. Stratford, Ontario is a restless, physical theatre where actors have to move all the time in order to share the lines out to different segments of the audience. It is difficult to play comedy as a consequence. Comedy requires the feed-line to be delivered clearly, while standing still. The laugh-line should be equally focused. Movement obscures it. Paradoxically, Ontario, which is an attempt at a Shakespearean theatre, is actually not a good space for verbal complexity because it demands too much movement.

The Olivier auditorium at London's National Theatre is based on pure geometry. And there is the problem. Great theatres are imprecise and bend like people, or like a crowd gathering to watch an event; they are not geometric, never composed on straight lines. The Olivier is wonderful for debate and for argument; it is hopeless for understatement. Shaw's arguments thrive there but not Chekhov's sub-texts. Shakespeare contains both, so he works sporadically.

Practically every theatre built in the last fifty years is too big. Economics demand more and more seats. But actors cannot be made larger – only audiences. To register and understand the unspoken means that an auditorium cannot hold more than seven hundred people. Charge a price that reflects the actual costs for these seats and you will have an elitist audience of rich people and a dead theatre. A good audience is never made up of one class – poor or rich, young or old. It must be mixed. Once again the case for subsidy is inescapable. Old theatres, like the pre-1997 Royal Court or the RSC's Aldwych or Brook's antique ruin at Bouffes du Nord in Paris are all spaces where the actor and the audience became one. Old auditoriums are easier to play: they are usually impure geometrically and full of ghosts and dirt. We should treasure them.

Conclusion

*H*ow do we judge the theatre? What do we say when we find it acceptable? We use a formidable vocabulary: we find a performance 'true', a production 'convincing', an evening so filled with 'reality' that we forget ourselves.

All these words for truth of course express the paradox that we are seeing something that is not true at all. The actor is pretending; the set is not real; the words are predetermined by the playwright. But our praise is for the intensity of the deception. If it is acute enough, our imaginations will be freed, and we will have a great evening.

Reality on the stage is always a paradox. What is presented of course is never *real*: how could it be? Reality is unacceptable. We would not be moved if Titus Andronicus really cut his hand off. We all know that we are playing a game of make-believe, inspired by the playwright and expressed by some good actors. Our imaginations are engaged with the absorption and delight of children at play; and the play has to be true – which means never so exaggerated as to *prevent* belief. 'Play' is indeed what the theatre lives on – and by means of play, we can imagine one pillar to be the whole of Ancient Rome, or an actress in her thirties to be a teenage Juliet.

What is on stage must therefore provoke and support our imaginations so that we can create what is *said* to be on stage. Yet however intense the experience, we never, I believe, forget that we are in a theatre. Doctor Johnson's bracing words always reassure me as I begin the necessary deceptions involved in creating theatre: 'The truth is, that the spectators are always in their senses, and know, from the first act to the last, that the stage is only a stage, and that the players are only players'.

How to create this willing suspension of disbelief haunts everybody in the theatre. Over-the-top acting alienates an audience and drives them away. A character trying not to cry will be more moving than a character indulging his or her tears to the full. The over-emotional is repulsive. A little restraint allows the audience's imagination room to breathe.

So there is a theatre reality which is not reality, but which we understand, a contract with the performers to represent reality and to allow us to imagine it. This reality can be a dreadful imposition.

There is a story about Chekhov and Stanislavsky. One of the actors told Chekhov that Stanislavsky intended to have frogs croaking, the sound of dragonflies, and dogs barking on the stage. 'Why?' Chekhov asked with a note of dissatisfaction in his voice. 'It is realistic,' the actor replied. 'Realistic,' Chekhov repeated with a laugh, and after a slight pause he said: 'The stage is art. There is a canvas of Kramskoi [a famous Russian painter] in which he wonderfully depicts human faces. Suppose he eliminated the nose of one of these faces and substituted a real one. The nose will be *realistic* but the picture will be spoiled.'

The stage is art – but it is an art where the concrete emotion or the particular word provokes the imagination to understand the ambiguous and the intangible. This rich game of make-believe between audience and actor grows stronger and stronger as film dominates more of our lives. The camera records reality, and what it photographs in imaginative terms is inert. A picture on the screen is not perceived as other than it is. It may represent fantasy, but it is not fantasy, and its achievement is no spur to the imagination. What it is, it is.

The theatre can thank the cinema because the camera has helped the drama regain its old potency. A group of actors asks their audience to imagine, and the audience complies. It is therefore perhaps easier to play Shakespeare, Chekhov, Ibsen, Beckett or Shaw than it was fifty years ago. The metaphor is more easily allowed. But will the theatre exist to express it in the future? Not, in my view, unless it is subsidised.

We need theatre more than ever. We need it above all to express contradiction in an increasingly simplistic and commercialised society. But if we will not pay for it and cherish it, it will not be there. As a worker in the theatre, I am not, I hope, a bitter man, but I am a sad one. After the high hopes of my adolescence at the end of the war (the Welfare State, free education, universities for all, subsidy for the arts, the National Health Service), the years since have been marked by an increasing disillusionment with politics and with political parties. They can't and don't care about long-term issues. And encouraging children to enjoy a rich culture and providing art for them when they are adults *are* long-term issues. Even if politicians care individually about the arts, they don't collectively.

My life in the politics of subsidised theatre has therefore been complex and nearly always disheartening. In contrast, I have had the clarity and co-operation of the rehearsal process when I was actually directing a play. To find a way of expressing Shakespeare is an absolute and gives you courage. Whitehall is usually a fudge and induces despair.

When will we wake up to the riches that we are squandering? When will we realise that the arts are diminishing by neglect and that the expenditure of peanuts would save them? We need an Arts Trust with a national membership, that would cherish them as the National Trust has cherished our architectural heritage. There is not much time. Why does the government spend so much time, effort and money on not subsidising the arts? The public must ask the question for the sake of the future.

DATE DUE